LSU Press Paperback Original

"Bruce Bond is one of our generation's best poets."   —Laura Kasischke

In his new collection, *Blind Rain*, Bruce Bond transforms the known and the familiar into the surreal and the new. With spare, unadorned language, he explores what it is to be both bound to the world and yet free within that world, the way in which the imagination deepens our engagements and yet offers some measure of distance at the same time. Bond opens with several elegies, some of which concern the last days and death of his father. Later poems contemplate the power of imaginative response as compensation for loss, focusing on poetry, madness, and music. The work includes a long meditation, "The Return," that hinges on the double sense of the word "true" as suggesting both "the real" and "the loyal," and so participates, often through personal and cultural narrative, in a postmodern conversation about the power of returning as a way of grounding us ethically and emotionally to the world at hand.

"A moving tribute to the power of music and the sensual life of the mind."
   —Dorianne Laux

"No poet writes about music better than Bruce Bond, and there are not many who can, poem after poem, combine such lucidity with such lyrical intensity. *Blind Rain* is a triumph of a book, a realized pursuit of language that frames and limns the deeply felt and the elusive."   —Stephen Dunn

BRUCE BOND, a jazz and classical guitarist, is professor of English at University of North Texas and the author of five previous poetry collections—*Cinder, The Throats of Narcissus, Radiography, The Anteroom of Paradise,* and *Independence Days.*

Ian Bondsmith

Cover illustration:
"Thunder Storm," engraving by Arkady Pugachev

LOUISIANA STATE UNIVERSITY PRESS

Baton Rouge 70808

www.lsu.edu/lsupress

Printed in U.S.A.

Cover design by Laura Gleason

$16.95

ISBN 978-0-8071-3308-8

90000>

9 780807 133088

W9-CUG-181

2609901V00001B/302/P
LVОW062006261211
Printed in the USA
CPSIA information can be obtained at www.ICGtesting.com

BLIND RAIN

BLIND RAIN

Poems

BRUCE BOND

LOUISIANA STATE UNIVERSITY PRESS
BATON ROUGE

Published by Louisiana State University Press
Copyright © 2008 by Bruce Bond
All rights reserved
Manufactured in the United States of America
An LSU Press Paperback Original
First printing

Designer: Laura Roubique Gleason
Typeface: Whitman, text; Mrs. Eaves, display
Printer and binder: Thomson-Shore, Inc.

LIBRARY OF CONGRESS CATALOGING-IN-PUBLICATION DATA

Bond, Bruce, 1954–
  Blind rain : poems / Bruce Bond.
    p. cm.
  ISBN 978-0-8071-3308-8 (pbk. : alk. paper)
  I. Title.
  PS3552.O5943B56 2008
  811'.54—dc22

                                    2007026576

In Memoriam

George Cline Bond
(1920–2003)

Winifred Cammack Bond
(1921–2005)

CONTENTS

I. ANONYMITY

AFTERLIFE

If you find yourself staring in your sleep
the way a boy stares into a campfire
on a lake of ice, his head lit, eyes closed;

if how you come to love this place
is how you leave it, how you walk
through the window of a lonely movie;

if the fury in the highest leaves is a man
tearing at his bandages, fierce as joy;
or deep in the park of a lover's body,

if it starts to fill with a shiver of stars
and the river water swells to meet them;
if what we know of paradise is the taste

of salt weeping in our mouths;
if fathers in their frustration, their pride,
become the sons we cannot console,

the ones we feed our native language;
if the birds that crown the far spire,
the drooping flowers of its bells, are choirs

of ash thrown, suspended, thrown again,
and higher still, a moon made of scars,
if it burns inside a nimbus and chill;

if we truly are the children of something
yet to be born, truly the carriers of letters
sown deep in the satchels of our bellies;

if every step we take is more blind than imagined,
here where the dark opens the graves of books
and kneels to read, repeating, repeating.

WAKE

One day now since my father last tried to speak,
since the outer provinces of his body shut
down like small cities when the power goes,
just the enormity of starlight to guide them
on their cold journey into dawn. I am writing
at the edge of the other half of life, the part
without my father in it; I feel the strange

sure pull of the earth I walk here,
the polish of the grass, the distance between me
and my students who look up and wait
for my first questions, knowing so little
of my life, just as I know so little of theirs,
only a poem at a time to hold us together
like children before a fire in the woods.

These months I have heard him steadily
fading in my telephone, his breath gone
short, just the occasional brush of wind
and language, here and there an angry stutter
and release, the little sighs that resign themselves
to his own deep and smoldering basin,
his own coastal reaches tossing in their tides.

The living too leave their ghosts behind.
And his, clearly, always the first to rise.
Somewhere a fork beats a metal bowl;
a strip of bacon crackles like paper at Christmas.
These days moving from room to room
I feel the shadow of this house begin
to lengthen, to feed the other pools of dark.

It's a mystery still, how vast the valley
inside a body. Blood. It's what you hear
when you cover your ears, that far surf
where life first sprouted its legs and crawled
ashore to dry its tail in the morning sun.
It's what sparks beneath a small syringe,
a red gem brightening in a sting of air.

It's what calls you to a father's ragged breathing.
Somewhere a lung fills with water.
Somewhere a great and weary muscle
beats the tender drum of the sky.
It's the father who knocks on the door
at daybreak, the knock that says, it's time
son, rise and shine, it's time to go, it's time.

Rehearsals for the New Order

The courthouse is empty now, ablaze
with holly, wreathed and ribboned for the season,
standing firm against a thrill of breezes,
the grinding arcs of stars, grackles crazed
and dizzying the turret, the drunken hair
of winter gardens at its feet, while inside
great mahogany walls, no judge presides,
no footstep polishes the marble stair,
no clerk turns to the window, rubs his eyes
and turns again: time to free the animals
into the evening air, to let them howl
from yard to yard; somewhere a solitary
stem of smoke blossoms from a chimney;
an old man watches his money wither
and rise, then fall again, over and over
without peace; somewhere a nation moves;
the blades of ships are opening the water;
somewhere a small tree brittles in its silver
and glass; all night we feel the sky there
listening, the tap that drips like tiny hooves.

The Invisible

In every body, if you dig
hard enough and long,
you hear the heart's footsteps
move from wall to wall,
down among the chambers
of the namelessly buried;

or out beneath nocturnal pools
of empty storefronts,
their televisions mute and flashing,
you hear a pulse that walks
the maze of boulevards
and sour alleys, the sighs

of buses expelling little flocks
of coats, each one thrown
to the anonymity of the next
dark step, lost in the dim
corner of our century, each
a shadow to the no one there.

In time a body grows weary
of its longing for the invisible,
its labor to be invisible
among them; in time the hour
like an abandoned cigarette
lit and clinging to its ash

gives in to the mercy
of gravity and silence,
which is when it arrives,
that brief sensation, uninvited,

small in voice and stature
though not without its hunger,

a chill like the tiny teeth
of stars, the physical greed
of being, here, ever more
helplessly here, here,
or so the moment wants
to believe, no fleet of bombers

to worry the horizon,
nothing, says this feeling,
not even the sting of denial
or desert sand, coming or going
no windy banner, no sun,
no shore, no hope of return.

FLAG

These nights in all their smoke
and armor, the great concussions

of bad faith thumping the horizon,
the epileptic flash inside the cloud

giving it depth, reach, weight to pull
as we move about our drowsy city,

I keep seeing my mother's room
at dusk, small, fading, lit by the ice

of television glass; how brief a life,
how long the hours, how fretful

the mother who picks the spice
grain by grain from a plate of meat,

who presses her palms against her eyes
as if to bury the world in the world.

Any wonder I too turn the pages
of my linens, bathed in ink,

that I sink my face in my pillow
and read. And whose world is it

that leans so close to blow out
the stray candles of my words,

to pare the evening horror down
to human size, to the crumpling

sound of spring rain; whose hand is this
that cracks the window of a book,

its Buddha hemmed in flags of fire,
a hub in the mind's wide *wheel* of fire.

Be in the world but not of it,
says the book—or is it the other way—

be lodged in the ring of flames
so deep there's no retreating.

I could be somewhere between this
wakefulness and another country,

in the no-fly zone of near-sleep
where ceilings buckle, sigh, click

into place, where the clock bleeds
a little night-light, humming,

where over and over the wind gives
its briefing to the alders,

and who am I to talk, I say,
as if God burned the letters that we sent.

My flag is not my flag
draped on the face of a tyrant statue.

Its colors are no brighter
than a song I sang badly as a boy.

No song, says the world, *not now.*
No mooning over a troubled covenant.

No song for the beast of the literal
heart thrashing in its irons.

And then it comes to me:
my father's weariness at the end

of day, eyes glazed, his body
bearing what I could not fathom.

It is 1954; somewhere still
ash settles on a village in Korea.

Bombs shake the Nevada sand.
Birds drop out of the sky in cinders.

Be in the world but not of it,
says the body, the eye, the ring of flames.

My father blankets the grass,
tunes the somber radio and falls

asleep, drowned in violins—
hello in there, we whisper—

that gentle snore like a cleft chain
dragging across the ocean floor.

LUGGAGE

Another jet's incision, a fire-blue sky,
another giant branch broken by the snow,
another thing I never said to him,
the sun of the heart crowning the horizon,
unsure if it is setting or rising.

Another hour, another souvenir,
an arm of ice attaching to our window,
and us here at the funeral feast
moving slow up the ladders of our ribs
to lift our heads and look,

to slip it in, the scarred world,
how it unclips its billowy laundry, folds it
into the eye, the skull, the heaven
we watch like someone else's luggage,
someone who got lost along the way,

whose one bag circles the carousel
as if to say, *go ahead, take me,*
I'm no one's if not yours now,
kneel down and grab my battered handle,
break the endless circle that I'm in.

ANONYMITY

Last night belonged to my father's memory
buried beneath a mound of shattered glass.

When I woke, it mended like so much water.
If I was weeping, it was nothing, I tell you.

It's like trying to catch the rain in your teeth.

I want to say words are never lifeless.
To speak is to stir the air beneath the wing.

Some trees flap with all the futility
of a dreaming child. It strips them clean.

The day he fell the heavy flood of the skylight
drenched our limbs, our shoulders, blurred our eyes.

For a while we were all of us strangers.
Now and then voices, an autumn of hands.

The vigilant machines of the ICU
dissected the silence with their soft clicks.

If you are wondering whether he heard us
as we hovered, you are not alone.

I am told the island of the moment,
unremembering, without a future

to whiten the still lip of the shore, is
our lightest happiness. Or painfully near.

When the man emerged from months of sleep,
the world burned with the tar of where he'd been.

Last night so many bodies walked in and out
of my dream, I, we, kept losing count.

I say this believing, as I once read,
we live forward, we know in reverse.

And so the awe of our tearing apart.
When he finally opened his eyes again,

the slow accumulation of ghosts returned:
the ache of a curve that refused to close.

How I thought his demise would make mine
less somehow, give it a father, a face.

How I thought it would get easier, to think
he had blazed that thicket that was his

final year, his breath a rope he cast out
to pull us all to the next needful thing.

Such dire work, raising the drowsy lid
of the mind to let the daylight in.

Outside, the small mercies of the lemon,
the fig, the prayer bead of a single wasp.

Fork, he said, sluggishly, without pride,
the silver of the one clear word grazing his tongue.

The day he died his name rested a little
deeper in us, chiseled in its bed of stone.

Last night I swore it was no trick to know
the worst and be a home for the knowledge,

a spacious place with a fire in the center,
burning books. Only mortal, we say, only

the skull and folly we were born into
to drag up the middle of our life and down.

Only mourning hunger, this troubled midnight
and its cast of characters fading into the wings.

There are times I write when the whiteness
of the page is the shadow of death.

A cat follows me from room to room.
Everywhere the quiet violence of the new.

Father, what are these strangers to me now?

It could be a woman I passed in a hall once,
and suddenly she is walking right through me,

down the center of my namelessness where, look,
there's nothing to erase, just the smooth

path like the punished floor of a river,
the flagstones gazing up at the sun, alive,

unknowing, doused in the cold and restless shine.

II. BLACK RADIUM

On Certainty

Emily winds her metronome
and lets it walk out of her hands.
She slips her fingers into the silent
glove of her first chord—skeptical,
meticulous. By now it's gone
on ahead into the thickening cadence,
through the voluptuous drizzle
in its path, held notes decaying
under the curved blades of slurs.

What is a piano, she thinks,
if not a brassy field at harvest,
an ebony mirror, a box of teeth?
What if not a harp asleep
in its coffin, ghost harp after harp
relinquished from its strings?
Somewhere a cathedral pours
a small welter of bells
through the ruffled measures.

She lets herself drag and rush,
swerve over the hills: to drift
is to resist. To surrender both hands,
hurl them as one music at another,
it's how she gives her body
to the difficult, how the difficult
refuses. Always the bored
puzzle of the clock before her,
the drowsy labor of its one
red spoke. No end in sight.

Only the departures that are everywhere,
the voices high as scarves
blown from a pleasure cruiser,
the tallest chords she tips
in place, how they soften
under their own cruel weight.
A note calls back the one before it,
the ones below. Soon
the ends of her arms burst
into the flames of second guesses.

She shakes her palms,
begins again from the double bar.
The way the metronome moves
you would think it traveled nothing
but an unbroken Euclidian line.
She hesitates, listens as it veers
with a slight stagger, nodding
off into silence. Still
she hears it step into the unlit
music in her hands, the spool
of its one eye, uncoiling.

LIBERATION OF DISSONANCE

Homage to Arnold Schoenberg

It's what he called his work, his *liberation,*
as if each note he heard might break the threads
of gravity, might burn a bit and darken
as he took his nightly walk, in his head

some hymn without a fulcrum, a native key.
And how Promethean it sounded then,
it sounds still, to take the giant tree
that is a tonal root and its extensions

and rip the thirsty tendrils from the planet.
But it wasn't so. Or if you called it
freedom, it was a vast and supple net
drifting, without center, perhaps, but not

without regime, as if one government
rose through the congress of another.
So bound to dissonance, so beauty-bent,
the tones spoke among themselves like numbers.

Sweet, yes. Unnerving, at first, especially;
though they undid themselves in the heat
of his insomnia, those nights his country
woke in smoke and sirens, a thing apart.

Or later as he stood on the sharp prow
dividing the exiled waters of his stare,
the red stamp of the passport (for now
at least) drowned in a still Atlantic of stars.

GLASS ENCLOSURE

Homage to Bud Powell

Who's to say the blow to his head was all
it took, the blister of a star that dawned
that time he stepped in to shield a friend,

if it was the billy club that nailed him
down or something older, more obscure,
a wound awakening night after night

until there was nothing to clarify
the sleep in him, no cell of the mind left
unstirred by the murmur of its neighbor.

You can see it in his photos, his eyes
narrow, shined with smoke, his head angled
as if expecting a nameless footstep,

a voice just over the ear's horizon.
Who's that playing? he once asked listening
to a cut of his own music. The closer he came

the newer the sound, the more refreshed
the hands that chased it. Leave it to the birds
of clusters to have a signature clarity there,

a prospect perched in the highest branches.
Those times he pulled a knife on the house cat
or hid trembling under a car, the big fists

of Largactyl and gin, how they nearly took
him over—it's why friends locked him once
in the crystal walls of a small apartment.

The only open door inside was the lid
to his baby grand. To think that room
could shed such grace, however troubled,

such jeweled and horizontal showers,
a bright wind thrown from the rock of the skull.
Closest intervals, he told himself, give

off the fiercest light, like an atom split,
a synapse ajar. However bitter the mother
of his boy, the child he became that could

not please her, however sad his own body
faithless in his arms, he kept going back, there,
to the black radium of the mind's piano.

Once he stood before a window for hours,
transfixed, and sang under his breath, *willow
weep for me,* as if he were walking

a thin wire of joy from tree to tree. *Weep,*
he sang, though the music, the way it swooped
and billowed, yielded a clearer stranger

picture flustered with leaves, with the flash
and tremor of their grip, their balance, a great
branch sweeping the broken glass of rain.

NERVAL'S LUTE

My sole star is dead,—and my constellated lute
Bears the black sun of Melancholia.
   —Gérard de Nerval

Walk into the black of Nerval's lute,
into the body of the instrument,
its choir of shivers, the gut of it lit
with language not quite spoken here, not yet,

with the loss of something so immediate
the memory eluded him: the mother,
the river, the woman who spurned him, not
them alone, but how they all would figure

into letters that he wrote the world.
And the world spoke in turn, though drenched
in music, in mercies of decaying pitch,
a foreign tongue which seemed the very will

embodied, the dream exhumed: everywhere
the votive candles of the lilies, the hills
of burning brass, the sky's acetylene stare
returning his those final days, his mind

in such a crushing fever the dead looked on
in pity, reached out even, so in the end
however disinherited the wound
of the open throat, however long

its stretch into the burial of suns,
it was a darkened happiness that dawned
that morning, that took him in its hands,
its human hands, and cut the body down.

North

Homage to Glenn Gould

1.

What he loved in the cold white meadow
of this, his northern province, what he found
in the constant powdering of snow
and silence was, if not his closest friends,
a nearness made of distance, a falling open,
as if the landscape were a cork-lined room
with a mike in the center, its ear pinned
to the slightest wing at the valley's rim,
the quietest branch, the deepest pulse.
A person's breath was a visible ghost
in the freeze here, it's true, but no less
in the Bach he recorded, his own voice
shadowing the music, like a man who tried,
take after take, to enter the sound he made.

2.

All the more surprising, his affection
for those winters, when you think of his hands
gloved in the bright of June, how he soaked them
in steamy ritual baths: the smallest hint
of wind bothering the air, and he knew,
as if his body had no skin to shroud it.
Once he played piano with a vacuum
cleaner going, cloaking how he sounded,
and he loved the way vibrations lit out
from the sensory world into something
more. Not to escape the body, not
wholly, but to feel inside it the strings

shuddering, to hear the music of the mind
in the flesh it lightens, the chill it sends.

3.

Sure, he had his answers, why he left
his life on tour, why the concert forum
was dead. Imagine, he wrote, the sweat
of thousands in the auditorium
penetrating one another's nostrils.
Which brings us back to Ontario:
the colder the country the less it smells.
Welcome, the silver age of the stereo.
And so he withdrew into the phone
conversations that consumed the night
with hardly a voice on the other line.
There were those who fell asleep a bit
to hear his words eroding in the black
stream, vanishing into music and back.

4.

As a child he had the gift of numbers,
not merely the ledgers of sticks and circles,
but the calculus of rain, the thunder's
mass divided by a flash of hail,
the chirping of May frogs at his window
raised to the power of clouds in April;
in short, he knew how certain measures go
to pieces, how they drug themselves and spill
into a kind of music. And what is music,
he wondered, if not the eros of equations

that erase themselves, that cannot make
a sound without opening a question,
that deepen their sleep in what little rest
he got, awake in his bedsheets, counting his breaths.

EXILE'S SONG

A boy lays his hands on the backs
of his mother's as they float
over the keys, over the startled
water of a dead man's music,
its small waves and minor scale
exhaling the way the sea exhales
though not without a soft strength,
the kind that nightly eats the shore;
the shadows of the mother's fingers
darken slightly as they touch
the living hand, so stiff, she tells
herself, unsure above the shallow
current—it's all leaving her,
she thinks, the lather, the pulse, the art
of moving with it, but she plays
this once, this final time, if only
to encourage the boy—and who can
blame her—the islands of his flesh
over hers, until she becomes
that place, for the moment, that hand
between the dead and the young,
between sky and the other face
of sky, as if it were the music
of the warm surge, its widow's lace,
that brings a child into the world.

BLUE INSTRUMENT

1.

It's come, the trembling time,
that tireless white noise moving
through her body, my mother's hands
so fitful in their quiet room, no music,

no books, no natural light, nothing
to graze her nerves with its cautious beauty,
save her ancient chest of drawers
watching over like a father. A curse,

she says, how they cannot understand.
In her mind a boat with no one in it
cast out over the night's lake, cloaked in fog.
Her face a lamp buried in the haze.

To speak of faith is to fail her, and yes,
I say, now is when you need it most.
The words go somewhere, I know; I see them
sink through the still waters of her eyes.

All I can do to take her hand in the strangeness
of my own, to be the fog around her,
the godless place inside the word *God,*
the wind of an arm, coming on, letting go.

2.

Somewhere my mother stopped playing
the piano and began to play the radio.
Even as her fingers knotted up with age
she felt the radio waves inside them.

Her whole body was one big radio,
first with the clarity of one song,
then two, then a blizzard of the many
ivories and voices, the all too sweet

and adolescent growl, the news flash
patter from the burning cities,
the chant of the blood beneath it all
thumping the floor like an angry neighbor,

the song of the worried keys, the rifled wallet,
the fool's joy in rainy weather, the hymn
of praise she buried in a book, here, now,
the one she clings to and will not open.

3.
Once I took my trouble to the river,
thinking how my mother's world
had contracted around her, its lord,
as surely as her body clung to the staff

that was her suffering. I took my image
of her on the throne of her bed
saying, don't go, don't chicken out now,
which is what I inevitably did,

or what I suspected of myself,
for I was part of that conspiracy
that could never be there, not fully.
Don't go, don't go, the echo marked time

as I went, thinking the river might calm
the mind with its constant leaving,
the cold amnesia of its shine, a flock
of clouds grazing upstream as I gazed

lost between a sense of solitude
and the weariness of traveling, always
with that one far voice, that one room
she could not leave for fear of being alone.

4.

No, she says, to the pill, the spoon,
the prayer, the fever, no to the sun
that hems a nervous curtain,
no to the cries of boys in a distant yard,

to the son's cruel talk of hope
and weather, no to the voice
that is not there, to the thousand ears
of leaves around her, no to the trip, the fly,

to the hired help arriving, sleepless,
worn by the call of a small gold bell,
no, she says with her head like the blind
musician sinking into a soft chord,

the kind of no that says, yes,
it's here, stronger than expected,
the bass of it opening up beneath you,
the hush that takes you with it as it fades.

5.

I used to dream of a blue instrument,
a dry breeze strumming the harp of the ear.
My mother too was there, the one
I never had, the musical mother,

her ghost rising out of the actual throat.
To think she lay there all along
inside the grip of bones guarding
its vital rhythms, inside the flush

of embarrassment or panic.
The unlived life is a far cry
from anywhere, a city on its floating docks,
its ships like constellations

over the breathing waters—the kind of stars
I steer by, even now as I think of her,
as I eat, sleep, move about,
forever losing my place in the sky.

III. TO THE SKYWALKERS

THE BEASTS OF PARADISE

Pity them, the way they graze,
their sun-drunk and leaden skulls
bowed to the meadow, to the pull

of the same dull page of grass,
the same polish of idiot clay
and seedlings jeweled with hornets,

fleas, stems of spit, the shredded
membranes of abandoned webs,
now and then a doleful lowing;

pity the long night in the coals
of their gaze, in the crops of nettles
brooding there, the muddy river

with the sky inside it, the cloud
with its gash of moonlight, closing;
pity the word that never climbs

the bruise-shade of the heavy tongue;
pity the hoof, the stumble, the sack
of blood and thirst that never sees

its own reflection in the water,
the one that stirs the mirror to drink;
pity the sex that burns its candle

in the open stars, the tender
folds of flesh with no language
sewn there, no leaf, no pride,

no blushing cloth like the one
a man wears to bed, the shade
his idle hour passes through

slow into his future garden,
a human path, he tells himself,
the way it lies down to meet him,

a rosy arbor at the threshold
trailing him in tatters, ruffling
its book, pity them, he says,

as they lumber off to slaughter
softly moaning, as he enters
autumn's grove with half-closed eyes.

GROVE

The things I do to wake just shy
of what I love, to keep from stepping through
the day into some dead heaven
of melancholia, no clouds, no wants,
no crackle of flags, just the blue
unmeasuring of hours to hold me
like a fly in the milk of southern Texas.

In time first mornings drift so far away
they crest the past horizon, at the rim
of what I can't remember. Which is why
I see in them such bright coins of early light
scattered by the olive trees. A child
kneels beneath their branches drawing
shapes of women in the dirt with a stick.

Each poor sketch is little but
a promise he keeps as he shuts
his eyes, the nearer the picture the more
distance he feels. Which is how
the figure of the child appears to me now,
how he lives, if he lives, far inside
the swollen boundaries of our native grove.

I carry this body as a fading portrait,
an heirloom from him to the last
unknowing. He has something to say still
if not to me to the image scratched
in the gathering shade, something
he says out loud, as if the silence
of things were their readiness, their ears.

Tonight boys cut their headlights
and coast under the sharpened stars.
They lightly stain the dark
with the smoke of their laughter.
Who would not dip again into skies
like this, into bowls of virtual
fountains we drank and lost our face to.

I want to say the silver at the bottom
is how I felt beside a girl once,
our beaded skins drying in the night air.
Slowly my shadow flew back
into my chest, feathering the buried
wings of lungs, and I repeated
her name for the pulse it made.

Who was that boy after all.
And when (the hand asks of every body
it explores) when will seasons mend
the difference between happiness
and olive trees, between sharpened stars
and pleasure; who will claim us
the way night claims an open window,
its vines unburdened, releasing their scent.

The Embalmer's Daughter Studies Ears

They became for her such sullen flowers,
what she tended in her palms
by the evening fire, after the last
chimes of cutlery and crystal,
when her father broke open
the toolbox of prosthetic parts,
its ready tray of awls and chisels,
the white translucent bricks of wax
that were his daily work.

So quick to yield, each molten coil
they sculpted into flesh, him there
in the crucible of their quiet time
to guide her through every groove
in the labyrinth, every rise and warble,
the fluid drooping of the lobe,
the dimple tucked at the rim
of the skull, at the pucker
of skin where the tiny stitches go.

Not quite, he would say, *not so
narrow,* the father in his voice
laughing softly, as she too laughed.
She raised her fingers over her own ear
to read the living text. Why
so many ridges, she wondered,
why this cup inside the cup,
this minor vestibule of air,
why this particular arc, this lip?

What god fell asleep at the pottery wheel,
facedown in the shallow dish

brimming with sweet nothings?
And yet, as she felt the bony wave
over the deepening, how it shields
and gathers, it seemed a thing of genius.
All day the vigilant shoreline
awash in the invisible waves;
all day the private pulse, dissolving.

So magnanimous, so withholding,
like the open door of a coffin
taking in the whispers as they pass.
Such troubled comfort: to see there
the plain mystery of the head, a father's
handiwork anointed in the final blush,
that hint of life laid over the surface
as if some sun had brushed the skin,
inquiring, and the blood warmed in answer.

ELEGY FOR THE LIVING

To look out at the scant snow
dusting the oaks and monkey grass,
falling through the eye of darkness

into the tentative grace of porch light
as if that light had kindled the air,
it struck me that a mother's mind

can be lost everywhere I look,
that the missing word on my mother's tongue
is one more place snow falls through,

and what I saw torn to ashes
in my yard, the sound of milk
pulled through the memory of milk,

kept calling at a constant remove,
ever the ground for the figure
which was absent now, from this day

always, though hopelessly expected,
the sky in the arms of trees gently
eating right out of their hands.

To the Skywalkers

Who hasn't felt the earth shudder
on its axis, to see them walk
the skeletal heights, these men

who weather a craze of breezes,
stepping from scaffolding to beam
and back, flagging the giant

girders down and starring them
with rivets. With every blue sizzle
and bite, a fainting spell of sparks.

Who hasn't wondered what it takes
to kneel over the great sky-well,
here and there a cinder of wings,

to know the opening beneath you
has you like a hunger. You listen
in vain for the hammer as it falls.

Doubtless they must feel sheltered
in their skins, quiet as a high
room cradled in the sound of rain.

The higher they are the lazier
the dark particles of strangers
gathered and swept from curb to curb.

A lesser man would dissolve
in the Pacific of what he sees.
Somewhere the startled gem

of a taxi turns and flashes.
Not that life is any cheaper
where they work. Anything but.

Only that they feel closer
not merely to the virginal sky
but to their bodies, like an exile

alone with his mother tongue,
turning to himself and singing.
It seems so deft, more cunning

than knives this faith, and older,
this gift of nerve that holds them
to their task: each eye is a child's

crystal clinging to its string.
It wakes them to the world they watch
time and again, forever waking,

until, that is, they descend
as the sun descends into their lives,
into night that falls between them

where they lie, face up on their pillows,
a black shaft above and below
to guide their every step of the way.

Terra Incognita

Then I look up to break
the spell of another history,
my eyes sore, near at hand

a shanty skyline of books,
pens, encrypted margins,
a field of sheaves, the dish

on my desk for our one deaf cat,
everywhere the flotsam
of ledgers and bad maps

however earnest, the unknown
seas to the farthest west
boiling with enormous snakes,

all the shadow-feathered
highlands and blue threads
mingling there as I lay

down my heavy volume,
set it on its face, a winged
creature locked in flight.

So many names tonight
crowned in blood and rubies
and God knows what . . . and me

with my lamp boring a small
dim hole into early hours
as if I were a prisoner of hours,

as if the still room swept
into emptiness and back
like an iron bell without a clapper.

So many stories like roads
that wear the language of flowers
that never bloom there.

And as I snap off the lamp,
as an animal starlight clouds the glass,
the kitchen path invites

again the body in need,
each soft step long rehearsed,
each print beneath my feet

dissolving: *tell me something,*
I say to myself, *make me*
a place for the mind to lie in.

And the dark opens its palms,
its untouched pages wet
and gleaming, a book of water

welling up with my father's
withered face; *tell me,* I say,
is there anyone there

at the bottom of the ocean.
And the face looks long and hard
from its stupor, an island

without tree or native language,
sand-white, then slowly sinking,
the socket of each eye filling up

with ink, hollow as a mouth.
And that is all. Which is when
a certain lightness comes

over me, unlikely as it seems,
as if I were sailing down
the edge of a cubical planet

into neither world nor sky,
deaf, sure, as any book,
any face harbored in the nameless

waters, any distant father's life
looking back, reading me.
A lie, I admit. Or something more

ambiguous. Unhistorical, at best,
like an ancient map I love:
this sense of someone watching

through the blue lens of unlived
hours. Read, read. *Here lie
monsters,* says the map. And then

a stillness. And the dark leans in
to kiss my eyes, to put out the tiny
lantern swinging in my head.

BLIND RAIN

Rare enough: the night that struck
so late in life, his eyes gone dark
white with age, the milk that blinds,
though stranger still: the way of the mind
as it too dimmed, how memory's map
dissolved beneath a fading lamp,
so even the arms of October
trees drew the stars into their embers,
and what hung above was the wet
slate of dreamless sleep, no west
to steer by, so little sense of here
there, though year after year
he scattered the net of his will
and reckoning—how fierce the world
in all its weather, the wind, yes,
which, as he listened, was the flesh
of many winds, the brittle rake
of a single leaf, a nervous gate,
the mindless ticking of the latch,
or now and then the black lash
of rain which, as he listened, was
many rains, the kind that sizzles
on the naked pavement, or taps
in a drunken stagger on the step,
the papery fluster of the hosta,
the vine, the nibbling of the grass,
the rickety marimba that is
a garden fence, its battered ribs,
and overhead the great elation
of oak thrashing in its constellation.
And so, in the rhythm of the sky
gone to pieces, he heard the shy

awakening of things, the sounds
settling over sounds, like hands
that read some long-forgotten face
in the distance, that softly trace
the lips that flinch there, cold, surprised,
the trembling of the closed eyes.

IV. THE RETURN

CRUCIFIX

Ever the lover with his torn cloth rippling
over his loins, that pallor an afterglow vaguely
translucent where he dangles, there, from a car

dash or chapel wall, over an unmade bed;
not that he is any less the figure of pain,
but rather that he is the Don Juan of pain—

ask any of his brides—that our worship is horribly
sweetened in pity, to see our maker at the mercy
of his creatures, even here centuries later

where divinity only prolongs his anguish,
tincturing the wild blood we hold to our lips,
careful with this death as if it were our own.

I keep thinking of a day on a stretch of highway,
that morning I glimpsed a fragment of a stranger
as they zipped a body bag over her face.

That too had radiance in it. I hold that face
like a candle afloat in a bowl of black water.
I keep straining my eyes for a closer look

the way I leaned before a painting as a boy
to see through the peephole in my savior's hand.
It could be anyone's fate in the diorama there

and is, anyone's curse. It could be one more slip
of the knife I'm using, and there in my palm
a strange eye begins to open, taking in the world.

TRANSPARENCIES

On a stone disk palette from ancient America
you see a carved hand with an eye in its palm,
sparked with sight, awakened there to hold us to it,

and ringed about the rim an afflatus of snakes,
their heads drawn back, tongues distended—they too are
    snakes—
so long they seem the body's lining blown inside out.

The whole mandala wavers still as if the eye
were the mind's island combed in vital tides
and poison were its power, the crown of being

lit up at the body's limit, keeping watch,
in the picture book of skin we read our lives in.

If you look into the stone's tiny flecks of lime
and mica, you can still make out the faded stain
of flesh-paint, still conjure a dim spectacle of hands

that worked the surface with chisels and pigments,
that wet their boar's hair brushes and tattoo needles
to illuminate the pages of their bodies, blood

rising to the color of blood, their skin littered
in a rash of eyes—less a second skin than a new
transparency, as if the needles made them more

permeable to naked sight. The prick of seeing
grazed the stone, zeroed in from eye to eye.

When I first saw Christ with an eye in his hand
it came as eerie comfort, to think he was less
alone out there, pinned to his cathedral wall,

his body pierced by the gazes of accusers.
It made me think of blood as light welling up
out of underworld rivers, or, if not light,

then the corporal water that lets it in: red
as the wound's iconography and swoon, the desert
drink passed among thieves and untouchables,

the color of breaking forth, emergency red,
the April garden littered with aches and blossoms.

Poor the mind that feels love for all mankind
and nothing but contempt for its neighbor.
Better to descend from the temples, to travel

the pipeline of the neck like drink itself, down
the furnace of the shoulder, its anger and char,
through rust-colored corridors to the world at hand.

I dreamt that as a boy. It didn't make me kinder,
wiser, this pressure of the body inside the body.
And I called up a portrait of a man giving sight,

as if some fire broke his skin, the inarticulate
flash of palms surrendering their phantom gold.

Any man's end has an eye at the center. Night
raises its giant hand and scoops back the body,
not lost exactly, but seeded in that ritual closure.

Never was flesh more the miracle-stranger,
never closer to the radiant gore of birth.
Out of the meaningless dirt the palettes of stone.

We come to a place where even rocks have a face
and back, a name to forget. Even rocks keep watch.
Somewhere below, a corpse sheds its blaze of worms

as if earth had pierced the insensible remains
to light them on their solitary journey.

MICROSCOPE

Some called it his retreat to the world,
how the boy with his mechanical eye bored
into smears of blood, mirror-lit, spellbound,
pin-prick angels congealing as he scrolled

his lenses to the stage. All of it true,
what they said, how the dawn of every new
sight trails a shadow of estrangement: you
never know until the moment, looking through

the stained glass, how vast the invisible
under your eyes. With every blushing cell
he sketched, the promise of a particle
inside each particle deepened like a well.

What child would scorn a body's greed
for light, as if he were a minor god
longing for passage back to solid ground,
to the island increment of life grown

distant over time. Who wouldn't pry
past the stray reflection of his gaze,
a one-eyed skeptic slouching where he prays
alone, turning ever inward. And away.

The Quick

I have just received *The Mystery*
    of Human Life, a pamphlet

from a lay believer who wants
    the Word to enter me,

to work its will the way the hand
    of God, pictured below,

enraptures the glove of a soul,
    a body, the things we say,

so that our outward selves might be
    His, heaven's puppets

blown to life with phantom voices.
    They speak low to some here

who scan the car crash of their lives,
    who chafe the broken

machinery of hope that pushes
    heavy hands from drink

to drink, hunger to hunger, who rip
    the phone from its socket,

not remembering why now, where
    it starts, this urge to stir

the quicksand of the daily ground,
    whatever that may be:

a stranger's bed, the nights we drag there,
  the thing, given the guile

and velvet of swamps, that swallows us
  faster the more we move.

And so the gradual temptation,
  days late in the thick

of the unspeakable, to practice
  the art of the corpse,

how quietly it lies, descending,
  even as the sea

of grass it enters, however slow,
  appears to rise.

THE RETURN

In memory of Giles Mitchell

As if the world we wake to,
glowing at the seams, were more
loyal than the one we leave,
more compelled, returning,
true, we say, as of a crime
or arrow, the path it takes,
the deadlier the truer,
the vision of a star pinned
and burning as the star goes out.

One more sleepless man at dawn
puts down his revolver,
closes it in his chest
of drawers. Its weight is that
of the moon sliding down,
an ache withdrawing
into the ephemera of days
to come. He chooses
with every breath and so lives

the burden, *free*, renewing
his allegiance step by step.
Who am I to presume the world
has a thing yet to tell him?
Still I want to say something,
as we all must, to recover
what it was that made life
the child he swore to spare, to care for,
to leave his minor fortune.

To recover, as in *the body*
recovered, the gold bullet
of the sun, all good things received
and covered, shrouded in light.
Long ago tomorrow was everything to me.
I loved it the way a small room
loves an only window,
the farthest reaches, the fever
of daylight as it rises and falls.

What is it to be so loosely in your skin,
so ill-defined who knows
what's there to give away?
Once, every wind blew its spiced and drunken rumors
through me. If I talked in my sleep,
it's just that I wasn't sure
if I was listening. Long ago
I loved the future the way a wick
loves the fire that eats it.

And so my first, my particular
flame, the girl whose bewildered
self emerged in the slow
shapes of deep water swells,
the kind that never break.
If not charity, then her distant
sister, that tentative step
and the sound it made, my ear
pressed to the rising sternum.

Not without our gaffs and stumbles,
those nights entangled

in the backs of cars,
the petty words that hung in the air
waiting for a mouth
to cover them up.
And all around us a wreath of crickets.
Going out, we called it,
the way a light goes out.

To throw a life into the life
you choose, into the one who chooses,
the mirrored mirror of the physical
eye, into the swift of not quite
knowing who, what, where
choice ends, the sea begins;
to make yourself a false promise
and watch the tidal rip of it
draw back into your aging eyes—

this too is one of those mornings,
how the surface of the screen
reappears at the movie's end,
though something more terrifying
is beginning and we know it,
something rising out of the body
looking down now on the plain
strangeness, the singularity,
of the body, our body, of anyone's body.

As children we could hardly look
to see our president wave, so slowly
pulled in his long convertible
splitting the cheer of a day in Texas.

Then that sound like a slapping
of books. The spits of flesh.
Over and over we watched it
as if the recurring footage might
reconcile a nation with its facts.

Anger, yes, and disbelief,
the blur of objects held too close,
but beyond that: it was the first
I saw my teacher as someone
more, history's orphan, closer
to a child, unsteady as she broke
the news, her voice so small,
so soft at times it seemed
she was speaking to herself.

Foolish as it sounds,
it was just then beginning to dawn,
not simply the flash of one broad day,
how it lowered a silence
the size of a cathedral,
but more: how the world that shook
my teacher and her brittle English
was, if not our world,
the frightened one we would inherit.

The first I heard of Vietnam
it was a television show my parents watched.
Me too as the time advanced,
as it fell in bolts of black cloth
over a family down the street.
Every morning the sun rose

on the jungle of who we thought we were,
what we lost, what we had become.
Even those who returned never returned.

What is more certain than the thing
of which we know so little?
Limousines drive the fresh dead
in caskets draped in fields of stars
so that the sky would drink up
the phantoms in their boxes,
calling them home, we say,
as if it were the living who live
as exiles in the new world.

Imagine the Tibetan children,
how the New China instructed them
to bring what each had killed
to school. It was their work:
one point for a fly, two a mouse,
three a bird, a cat, and so on,
anything to break the life cycle
of the heart, how they threw it
into each small suffering thing.

I don't pretend to know the luminous
emptiness of what they see,
to have what it takes to step lightly
through the labyrinth of Bardos
and back. Still I admire anyone
who, as the story goes, chooses
to return to life, whose kind ghost

reawakens, an infant in the flesh
of day, flushed and crying.

And looking down on all sides, the joy
of arrival. So quiet, this joy,
so easy to dispel with the need for joy,
I am reluctant now to speak of it.
For those who wait, it seems to come
from a great distance, returning the way
a father does after years at sea,
his too large coat and the hat he holds
doused in the indigent rain.

True, we say, as of one returning
but also of the eros of return.
Why is it always one woman now
balancing the scales of my bed?
My north, my wife, my nocturnal iris,
each night a little smaller
in her skin, she whom the curtain
turns to in its blindness.
So quick to fall asleep.

A gift, how faithfully she takes
the dishevelment of days
inside, expecting just as surely
to return, as if she saw it: the future
had arrived without closing its eyes,
its distance, as if anything so
shy, so alive, could be
before her, still and breathing,
calling her name.

WILL

To the locusts that blur the lyres of their shells,
I leave my blindness at the end of day.
To the distant whistle of the train at dusk,
I leave the smoke in a girl's hair.
To days I dipped my body in, I leave my only shadow.

To the gravel road where it crackles and spits,
to the fluster of the wheel, the brake,
the broken shoulder, its buckle and curve,
to the long labor of the open eye,
I leave one lush confession.

To the pincers of ants dismantling a bird,
I leave the bitter patch at the tip of my tongue.
To the porch light haloed in a scribble
of moths, I leave my boyish appetite.
To the hymn, the yawn, the three in the morning,

I leave the warmth of the engine
as it settles and purrs.
To the empty page beneath me where I lie,
I leave the weight of ink above.
To the hole that is my throat, I leave the flesh around it.

To the dream I can't remember,
I leave the one I won't. To my father's memory,
I leave the bread crumbs of my name.
To the body that follows a body to its grave,
I leave the seagull's laughter.

To the bride who says good-bye to the mirror,
I leave the cold face of the mirror.
To the one who reads, I leave the fire.
To the quiet brightening behind me as I go,
I leave the quiet to come.

Acknowledgments

The author would like to thank the editors of the following journals, where poems in this book first appeared:

Boulevard	"The Quick"
Brilliant Corners	"Glass Enclosure"
Cincinnati Review	"The Beasts of Paradise"
Colorado Review	"Afterlife"
Crab Orchard Review	"Transparencies"
Georgia Review	"Wake"
Gettysburg Review	"Crucifix"
Green Mountains Review	"To the Skywalkers"
Harvard Review	"The Invisible"
Indiana Review	"Elegy for the Living"
Iowa Review	"Anonymity"
Massachusetts Review	"Exile's Song"
New Orleans Review	"The Return"
Passages North	"The Embalmer's Daughter Studies Ears"
	"Grove"
Ploughshares	"Will"
Poetry	"On Certainty"
Prairie Schooner	"Luggage"
	"Terra Incognita"
Sewanee Review	"Blind Rain"
Southern Review	"Blue Instrument"
Southwest Review	"Rehearsals for the New Order"
32 Poems	"Microscope"
TriQuarterly	"Flag"
Western Humanities Review	"Liberation of Dissonance"
	"North"
Willow Springs	"Nerval's Lute"

"Transparencies" was reprinted in *Vespers: Contemporary American Poems of Religion and Spirituality* (University of Iowa Press). "To the Skywalkers" appeared in *Wild and Whirling Words* (Etruscan

Press). "On Certainty" appeared as part of the poem cycle "Incarnations" in the chapbook entitled *The Possible* (Gerald Cable Book Award, Silverfish Review Press). The poem was also included in the *Quarterly Review of Literature Poetry Series: 50th Anniversary Anthology*. "Liberation of Dissonance" was a featured poem in *Poetry Daily*. "Rehearsals for the New Order" was a featured poem in *Verse Daily*. "Terra Incognita" appeared in the anthology *Ghost of a Chance* (Helicon Nine Editions). The poems "Wake" and "The Return" were republished in *Poetry Southeast*. "Wake" was also republished in *Penguin Review*. The author would like to thank Austin Hummell, Corey Marks, Enid Shomer, and most especially Nicki Cohen for their invaluable wisdom and support during the writing of these poems.